SWING TRADING

A Strategic Guide to Swing Trading in Stocks, Options, and Futures for Beginners

Joey Thompson

outlined in this book.

By reading this document, the reader agrees that under no circumstances is the author responsible for any losses, direct or indirect, which are incurred as a result of the use of information contained within this document, including, but not limited to, — errors, omissions, or inaccuracies.

Table of Contents

INTRODUCTION

In the following chapters I will discuss everything that you need to know in order to get yourself started on swing trading and to make sure that you can bring in a lot of money in no time. There are a ton of great options that you can use when you want to invest your money, and there are even a number of other options that work on the stock market as well. but nothing will provide you with the same return on investment, and the same ease of use, as we can find when we work on swing trading.

This guidebook will take some time to talk about swing trading and all the steps that you need to follow to get started on this in no time. This is a great strategy to use that allows you to have a bit more time to wait for the big changes in a stock price, while still earning a good profit in a shorter amount of time compared to some of your other strategies.

To start our adventure, we are going to take a look at swing trading and some of the basics that it entails. We will look more at what swing trading is and then dive into some of the benefits of using this trading method over some of the others. We will even take a look at how this kind of investment strategy is different than day trading, though the two do have a lot of things in common.

When we are done with that, it is time to move on to some of the steps that you need to take, and some of the things that you need to consider when you are ready to make your first official trade in swing trading. Don't worry, this is a whole lot easier to work on than it may seem, and you can enter the market in no time once you have those basic steps down.

From that point, it is time to get into a few of the strategies that we need to follow in order to see success with the swing trading strategy. For starters, we need to focus a bit on the idea of the technical and the fundamental analysis. We will discuss these a bit throughout the whole guidebook because they are so important and can make a world of difference in the results that you can get, but we will take a few chapters to explore each of these on their own. This can help us to see the benefits of each and can make it easier to determine which one we should use for our trading.

Then it is time to move on to some of the different things that we need to know in order to use swing trading on the different securities. We will focus mainly on how to trade in stocks with this strategy, but it is possible to also work with options like futures, commodities, the Forex market, and more and still see some great results. We will take some time to discuss this through this guidebook.

Then we can end this guidebook with a discussion on some of the best options when you want to pick out a strategy. These strategies can help us out with knowing when to enter the market and when to exit, and they are used by beginners and professionals in this market all of the time. We will look at some of the most common strategies, so you are set to get the best out of this process in no time.

This may seem like a lot of information when we first get started with the swing trading market. But this is also a really profitable way for us to learn how to invest and make money on the market as some trends like to change. It is one of the most efficient methods of trading, and it comes with the lowest amount of risk as well. when you are ready to learn more about swing trading and how you can use it to make money as well, make sure to check out this guidebook to get started.

There are plenty of books on this subject on the market, thanks again for choosing this one! Every effort was made to ensure it is full of as much useful information as possible, please enjoy!

CHAPTER 1

HOW TO GET STARTED IN SWING TRADING

Investing is a great way to take your money and make it grow. And if you get down the right strategy and learn how to make this work for you, you will be able to get some really great return on investment without having to work on it full time. There are actually quite a few options when it is time to invest, and you are sure to find the one that works the best for you in no time. But one of the best options that will help you to earn a lot of money in a short amount of time, but is not as risky or as stressful as day trading, includes a method known as swing trading.

What Is Swing Trading

We first need to take a look at swing trading and what this is all about. To start, swing trading is a style of trading that we can use to capture the gains that happen in a stock or any other financial security that we want to use, over a period of a few days to several weeks. These traders are going to work with technical analysis to help them find the right opportunities for trading and to help them make some more money. There are times when the fundamental analysis is a better choice for the swing trader because it allows them a new way to look at the patterns and the trends in prices.

Both of this analysis is going to be important. But they do work in completely different ways, so we have to understand when to use each one. The good news is that we will talk about both of these and how each one works later on in this guidebook so you can get the best results with this in no time.

This is just the start of what we need to know to start with swing trading; there is so much more that we can focus on as well. for the most part, the process of swing trading will involve holding onto a position, doing so either long or short, for more than one trading session. This is the difference between swing trading and day trading. The day trader will purchase security and has to sell it by the end of the day. The swing trader is still on a short term strategy, but they can have anywhere from two days to two weeks to decide to hold onto the stock or to sell it for a profit or a loss.

The swing trader gets a little bit more time to work with the stocks than a day trader, but they usually need to get rid of the stocks, either for a profit or a loss, within a few weeks. There are some trades that last for a few months and can follow this option, but it is important that you only hold onto the stocks for a short amount of time before doing this strategy. Holding onto them for months or years turns you out of swing trading and over to some of the other options. Those are great ways to invest as well, and if you want to mix it up sometimes, holding onto stocks for longer can work well too, but this is not swing trading.

In a few cases, a swing trade can start out with us planning to use it for a few days, and then we get out of the trade during the same trading session. This is a rare option, and usually, the swing trader will only use it when the conditions are really volatile, and it is hard to know where they will go after this

The goal of working with swing trading is that we want to go through and capture a chunk of a price move we think will happen in the future. While there are some traders who like to look for stocks with a lot of volatility in them, some others like to work with a stock that is more sedated. No matter which one you choose to go with, the process that comes with swing trading asks us to identify where the price of the asset is most likely to move next, entering into a position based on that information and then getting some of the profits from that move if it does show up.

Most successful swing traders are only looking to capture a bit of the potential price movement. Then they are ready to get out of the trade before things reverse, and then move on to the next opportunity that comes out there. As you learn how to read charts better and understand more about the stock market or the security market that you want to work with, you will get better at handling some of the ups and downs of the market, and you can make some good decisions on how to do your trades.

There are a few things that we can consider when it comes to working with swing trading, and that we need to review before we go through with some more information on swing trading and what we can do with it. These points will include:

1. This kind of trading will involve the trader taking some trades that will last a few days up to a few months to help the trader make some profits from the price moves that they anticipate.
2. Swing trading is a good way to trade, but the trader has to be ready to see that there are risks for staying in the market over the weekend and overnight if they choose this strategy. It is

possible that the price cold gap and open at a really different price by the next day or after the weekend.

3. Swing traders are able to take some profits with the help of the risk to reward ratio based on the profit target and the stop loss, or they are able to take some losses or profits based on some of the price action movements or the technical indicators along the way.

Swing trading is often seen as one of the most popular forms of trading because there is a lot of potential profit that can be made out of it. This option allows the trader to look for some opportunities that will show up within a few weeks, and then they can capitalize on it. This can make some good money in the short term, without being as risky and volatile as getting in and out of the market quickly with day trading.

If you decide that swing trading is the right option for you, then you should have a really good familiarity and understanding of how technical analysis works. We will talk about some of the specifics that come with this option later, but basically, it involves looking at lots of different charts and figuring out the best course of action based on some of the trends that show up in the market. Adding a bit of knowledge about the news and how that can affect the stocks and whether that will keep things following the trends or disrupting them, can make a difference in how much success you can see with this kind of trading.

Many traders who use this strategy are going to assess the trades based on the risk to reward ratio that shows up with this one. When they are able to take the time to analyze the chart of one of the assets they are interested in, they can then determine where they will enter the market, where they would like to place the stop losses, and then they can anticipate the likely profit they will make if the trade goes their way.

We have to really think through some of these trades to get the best deal. If you are risking $1 a share on a setup that is likely going to give you $3 in profit, this is going to be favorable in terms of the risk and reward you are taking. If you are doing this and the reward is only $1 or even lower, then this is not a good option to work with. You need to be reasonable with this. What is the likelihood that you will get the profits that you want, without being unreasonable in the process?

Most swing traders like to work with technical analysis because there are some short-term natures that come with the trades. This is important to learn how to do, but sometimes a fundamental part added into it is a good idea as well because it enhances the analysis that you can get. For example, if a swing trader is taking a look at things and notices that there is a bullish setup in the stock, then they may ais want to verify that the fundamentals of the asset are looking favorable at the same time.

Swing traders will often take some time to look at the daily charts and see whether there are some good opportunities that they can jump on. It is common that they can look at the hour or the 15-minute charts to see whether there is something for them to jump on, and it can help them to find the right stop loss, take profit, and entry levels that will make them the most money possible.

There are a few benefits and negatives that we can see when we look at swing trading. We will take a look at some of the positives first:

1. This will require less of your time than day trading and can give you more profits with less work.
2. It helps us to maximize some of the short-term profit potentials because it is easier to catch some of the market swings that happen.
3. It is possible to work just with a technical analysis of this one and see some great profits out of it. When we only have to work with one type of analysis, it is a lot easier to trade and can make the process easier.

While there are a number of benefits to working with swing trading, we also need to focus on some of the reasons why people are warry about using this kind of trading strategy at all. Some of the negatives that come with swing trading include:

1. Some of the positions that you use will be subject to risks that occur overnight and on the weekends. This can make it a lot riskier to get the work done.

2. If the market does a big reversal on you, this can create big losses that are hard to work with.

3. Sometimes a swing trader will miss out on some of the longer-term trends because they are focusing just on the short-term market moves that they see

How Is Swing Trading Different From Day Trading

If you have spent some time learning about day trading in the past, you may feel like there are a lot of similarities that show up between the two trading strategies. There are a few differences that show up

here, but there are also a few things that can make this kind of trading similar, and as a beginner, it is hard to know the similarities and the differences between these two styles of trading.

The main difference that shows up between the swing trading and the day trading is the amount of time you spend in the market and hold your position. With swing trading, you will hold onto the position at least overnight, and often for a few days and then you will close out the position. The day trader is going to close out their position before the market has a chance to close on the same day they purchase the security. So, to keep it simple, day traders will purchase and sell their positions in one day, and then the swing trader will hold onto the position for up to a few weeks.

Because they hold onto the position overnight, it is likely the swing trader will have to deal with some form of unpredictability from the overnight risk. This could be things like gaps and a down against the position. By taking on the overnight risk, these trades are made with some smaller position sizes compared to what we see with day trading, making the assumption that the two traders would have the same sized account. The day trader is more likely to work with position sizes that are larger because they can take that risk out.

A swing trader is going to also have some access to margin or leverage up to 50 percent. This means that if the trader has been approved to do something known as margin trading, they would only need to have $25,000 of their own capital to make the trade, but the margin would allow them to trade up to $50,000.

Tactics to Use With Swing Trading

There are a lot of great tactics that a swing trader is able to utilize to get the best results. We will look at a few of these in more detail at the end of this guidebook, but we can certainly look at a few of the basics now and see how this works. To start, it is common for a swing trader to look at multi-day chart patterns. Some of the common patterns that they will look at including the average crossovers, the head, and shoulders patterns, cup and handle patterns, triangles, and flags. The choice you make in a strategy is going to depend on how the market is working and what seems to make the best sense for your trades.

Each swing trader who gets into the market has to come up with their own plan and strategy that provides them an edge over other traders. This will involve looking for trade setups that can lead to movements that are predictable in the price of the asset. This is not an easy thing to work on, and there isn't a single setup or strategy out there that is going to behave and work each time that you use it.

The good news is that if you work with a good risk and reward ratio, then it isn't necessary to win each time in order to get ahead. The more favorable the risk to reward strategy, the fewer times that you need it to win in order to get the profit that you want overall in many of your trades.

The Benefits of Swing Trading

Before we end this chapter, we need to take a quick look at some of the benefits that you can get when you decide to use swing trading as your method of trading overall. There are a lot of options for investing, and they can all provide you with some benefits and some reasons as to why you should use this one over one of the other choices. But there are a ton of benefits as to why swing trading is the best one here, and why you should at least consider adding it to your toolbelt if you want to be successful here.

Some of the benefits that you can enjoy when it comes to swing trading include:

1. It is easy to work with: if you have never done any kind of investing before, you may be pleasantly surprised at how easy swing trading in the stock market can be. It doesn't take as much work as some of the other options, and as long as you can look over the stocks and the trends that come with the many charts you

should be looking over, you will be able to start this up without a lot of problems either.

2. It doesn't require a lot of money to get started: Of course, the more money that you can safely invest in the market, the more that you can potentially earn. But even if you just have a little bit of money, you will find that this will work out well. this is a great starting point for those who have been trying to get into some kind of investment but don't have a ton of money to spare in the process.

3. It has less risk than other options. Compared to working with day trading and even some of the other types of investments out there, swing trading can carry much less risk. It provides us with a good amount of profit for a lot less risk, so that is positive for each investor who would like to give it a try.

4. It can work on any stock or security. You will also find that when you work a bit with swing trading, it is a fantastic way for us to make some good profits whether we work with the stock market or with some other type of security. We will speed most of this guidebook talking about how to use this in relation to the stock market, but a lot of the information can be changed to work with other securities as well. this gives you some freedom to try different things.

5. It can bring in quite a bit of profit: If you do this well, and you take the time to really learn about the stocks and what they have to offer along the way, there is a ton of potential to make money on these kinds of trades. This is not a get rich quick kind of scheme, and you will have to stick with it and put in some work if you would like to turn this into a viable way to make some money or an income, but it is a lot easier than spending hours at work hoping to get a raise.

As we can see here, there are a lot of reasons why someone would want to consider working with swing trading and making this a big part of their process as well. When you can take a look at some of the charts and graphs that come with it, and you pay attention to the trends and what they are saying, you will find that this is one of the best ways to make money in the stock market.

CHAPTER 2

HOW TO PREPARE FOR YOUR FIRST TRADE

Now that we have had some time to learn more about swing trading and what it entails, it is time for us to move on and learn a bit more about how to actually enter into a trade like this and how we can do it well so that we make some profits. This process does have a few steps that we should spend our time on, but it is not difficult. Once you set up your own account and find a good broker who can walk you through all of this, you will find that the process is as simple as can be. Some of the steps that you can take when it is time to prepare for our very first trade as a swing trader includes:

Find a Good Broker

One of the important decisions that you will make when you first get started in trading is who you will hire as your broker. This is a really important decision and one that you need to take some time, and perform some research on, to make sure that you are prepared and will have the right one. There are many brokers out there, so this can be a hard decision.

The first thing to determine is how much time you plan to put into your investing, and how much help you will need. Some people like to do the work all on their own, and others will need some hand-holding to get them started at least. There are brokers out there that can help with both situations; you just need to know what your situation is before you start looking.

Then you need to take a look at some of the fees that the broker is going to charge. If the fees are too high, then they will start to eat into your profits, and that is never a good thing. All brokers are going to charge you some fees in order to invest and use them, so that is something you should expect right from the beginning. However, the way they charge these fees, and the amount that you spend on these fees over time is going to really depend on each individual broker.

Some will charge you for each transaction you do. This can work well for some of the long-term investments because you won't move your position all that much during that time. But as a swing trader, it is likely that you will make a lot of trades on a regular basis, so this may add up quickly. Others will charge you based on a percent of how much you make as you go through the process.

There isn't a right or wrong way that the brokers will charge their fees to you, but you do need to be careful and know how this is done before you jump in. talk to your broker about this ahead of time because you do not want to be surprised by the fees and some of the other parts that you weren't aware of after you enter the trades.

You can also take some time to look more at some of the features and special incentives that the broker is going to offer to you. These will change based on the broker you want to use, but they can be a great way to get you ahead and are offered just because the broker is trying to get some new clients through the door. This is beneficial for you, so you might as well use it at least a little bit.

And finally, it is often a good idea to go through and talk with your broker, at least a little bit. This will make it easier to get to know them and figure out if their style is similar to yours. If you don't feel comfortable with one broker over another, then this is a good sign that you should choose someone else. You could be with this broker for a long period of time if things work out, so you need to be comfortable with using them as well.

Decide How Much You Can Spend

This is a tricky one to work with because the amount will depend on your own personal budget. Any amount can be used to make trading profitable. But you do have to keep in mind to never trade more than you can afford to lose. Too many new traders will just throw some money into the market, assuming that they will get rich in a few weeks and get their money back in no time. And then they make the wrong decisions about trading and lose all of that money, money that they really had needed for something else.

That is one of the number one rules that we have to follow when it comes to trading is to never use money that we can't afford to lose. This may seem silly and may keep us back from purchasing as many stocks as we would like, but it is one way to limit the amount of risk that we take on with swing trading. And swing trading, just like other forms of trading and investing, does carry some risk.

One way to make sure that you follow this rule is to set up a separate account that you would like to use just for trading money. Each month, add in the amount that you can safely invest, without hurting your other finances, and that is all that you can trade on. That way, if you make a few bad trades, you have not lost all of the money that you need for making the house payment or something else that needs to be paid that month.

Do Some Research

Research is your best friend when you go through this process. The more time that you can spend researching and look at charts, the more that you will understand how the market works and how much you can make on it in the process. No one has done well in the stock market, no matter what their strategy is, without first doing some research to help them out here.

There are a number of sources that you can use in order to get your research done and to make sure that you really like the results at the end in terms of profits. Charts and graphs about the stock market, and about the particular security that you want to spend time on will be your first source. Swing traders like to spend a lot of time working with technical analysis, so these charts and graphs are going to be so important in your work.

In addition to these charts, there are a few other resources that you can spend your time on to make sure that you see the best results and that you can really take your trading to the next level. News sources are a good place to start because they can provide you with some really great information that the company is releasing or what other analysts are saying as well. Then you can also look at some of the financial records of the company to see whether it is in good standing and is likely to play along with your plan for as long as you need it too.

There are a lot of benefits that come with working on swing trading, but you need to have a plan in place, and you need to make sure that you have done your research. There is a lot that can happen on the stock market in a short amount of time, so being prepared and making sure that you know what is going on with your chosen companies can help you to see more profits.

Find Some Good News Sources to Use

While the technical analysis is a good option to use, and lots of charts will become your best friends when going through this process, you should also consider looking through some news sources, ones that you trust, and can keep you up to date on a regular basis. You will become best friends with these, and they can guide a lot of the trades that you want to do.

Sometimes, the big swings that you see in the market the ones that will make swing trading more successful than other types of trades are the ones that are based on news that a company releases about itself. This news can make a difference in which stocks and securities that you would like to purchase, and if you know that these releases are about to come out, you can use this to your advantage to get ahead and make some good profit.

Let's say that you are reading the news and you see that Company A is about to do a big expansion in the area. They will add new jobs and some new products that you think will sell really great. You may see that this is all about to be released in the next few weeks. You may make the prediction that once the company releases all of this information and shares it with stockholders and others, it will make the value of the company go up and raise its stocks.

So, with that information in hand, you go to your broker and take a look. You notice that the stock price is doing well and has for some time, but you are predicting that it is going to rise really high in the next few weeks or so as others start to take a bigger interest in this company and what it has to offer. If the risk to reward ratio that you calculate out makes sense, then you purchase as many of that stock as you can and hold onto it.

If you were right, the company, sometime in the next few weeks, will release information to the public, and the public will go wild. Everyone will want to be a part of the changes that Company A is introducing, and they will purchase up the stock. Now the price of the stock starts to rise really quickly because the demand is a lot higher. When it finally gets to the point where you feel comfortable making a profit, you will sell off your shares and pocket the difference.

This is a really successful method to use when you want to work on swing trading. It will allow you a chance to go through and get into the market and make a purchase before the price goes up, and then you can sell when the price is high. You have to work with some really reputable news sources, and you have to be able to catch some of the smaller items that are in those news sources to make sure that you can make the most profit possible.

Consider the Good Risk to Reward for Your Trade

It is so important that you come up with a good risk to reward ratio for any trades that you complete. And this risk to reward ratio has to make sense. You will not be able to make $100,000 on a trade unless you have millions to invest in the stock. The stocks are not likely to go up that much in just a few weeks, so get that idea out of your head right now. However, you can make $100,000 a year on these trades, though you will have to do them over and over again during the year if you have the right risk to reward ratio.

As we mentioned a bit in the previous chapter, a good risk to reward ratio would be if you spent $1 on a stock, and you thought this trade could potentially bring you $3. The risk is higher than the potential loss that you could suffer, so it is a good one to use, especially if it looks pretty certain that the market will move in the direction that you want.

On the other side of things, if you put the money into the market and your reward was only $.50 for the $1 that you spent, it is likely that this is going to be too risky to work with. We want the reward to be as high as possible compared to the risk that we take. This helps us to make some good profits, with less risk, even if the stocks don't go up as high as we would like.

When you take a look at a few of the charts and other things that are important to this process, you need to make sure that you look closely at the risk to reward ratio that you will deal with. This can change based on which stocks you are following and what kind of trade you would like to do. But before you enter into the trade, you need to know pretty well whether this trade is going to be worth your time or not.

Completing the First Trade

Now that we have taken some time to go through the other steps, it is time to actually complete your first trade. Make sure that you already have the money you would like to spend on trading in your account. This usually takes a few days to process, so having it set up and ready to go inside of your account can help you to start trading right away. Do this while working on some of the research and deciding all the other parts.

By this time, you should already have a good idea of which stocks are going to be the ones that you would like to purchase. When the stocks reach a point that seems like a good discount, or at least will provide you with the reward ratio that you want if the trend goes in your direction, then it is time to make the purchase and get the number of stocks that you want.

Decide on the entry price that you want to use. How much are you willing to spend on each stock from the start? How much do you think the stocks will go up in the direction that you want? This will tell you how much reward you can make in the process. Your research should tell you a reasonable price that you can get for the stocks, so consider that when you pick out an entry point. It would be nice to get a deep discount on a stock, but that is just not possible in these kinds of trades most of the time. You should be able to tell what the low point, or even the average, is for this stock, and then your goal is to purchase close to that.

Before you enter into the trade, it is time to make some decisions on what your stop-loss points are. You need to have one in place for how you will get out if things take a turn for the worse and you start losing profit. And you need one in place for when you start making profits.

With swing trading, you will often jump in early and get some stocks for a discount before others do, and before a big event. This event may be temporary, and the price of the stock may neutralize a bit and can even go back down. This is why the stop loss for profits is important. It will make sure that you take the profits and get out of the market before you lose everything that you earned.

A stop loss to prevent you from losing too much money is important here as well. this will ensure that when the trend goes opposite of what you had estimated, you will get out of the game and limit your risks. You can decide how much risk you are willing to take, and how much money you would be willing to lose. But the best bet is to set this ahead of time before the emotions can get into the game and mess up your plans.

Most brokers online will make it simple to do this process. You can look up the stock, click on a button that says buy or purchase. When you get there, decide how many of the stock you would like to purchase. This depends on how much money you are willing to invest and how much the stock costs. Agree to the market value and click submit.

The trade is going to usually happen in real-time, though if there is a lot of volatility or something else going on, then it can take a few minutes to finish up.

Once that is done, then you are in the market. It is important that you take the time to watch the market and see what it does. The market will have a lot of ups and downs over the next few days, so don't worry if you see some profits lost during this because it will most likely bounce up unless there is a big change in the market or in the company.

You should know about when the big event is going to happen that you want to capitalize on, so that should help here. But there can be some unexpected changes that creep up on a regular basis, so it is always a good idea to watch the stocks and see what they do. If something goes the wrong way or doesn't act how you thought it would, then it is time to get out of the market and try something new.

The goal here, if you did all of the research well and you made sure that your risk and reward were at a good ratio, then you will be able to get out of the market at the right time to make some good profits. You will not get rich off one trade though, even with the possibility of making some good money, so take that off the table right now. Thinking about this logically and understanding that you need to put in some work and do the swing trading many times to become rich, will help to keep your emotions in check and will make your trades more successful.

And that is the process that you need to follow to get started with swing trading! You will just rinse and repeat, doing this over and over again, and putting in the right safeguards to make sure that your money is as safe and possible through all of this. When that comes together, you can start to make a good profit with swing trading, and you will get a whole lot better at it in the process as well.

CHAPTER 3

THE TECHNICAL ANALYSIS

There are two main types of analysis that we can do when it is time to enter into swing trading, or really any kind of trading for that matter. We have mentioned them a little bit before and introduced them as the technical analysis and fundamental analysis. Now it is time for us to go into some more details about what these are and how they work, so we can utilize them for some of our needs as we enter into the market. You will see that these two types of analysis peak out for any kind of investment that you do in the stock market or with other securities, so learning them now can help you if you decide to branch out to other types of investments later.

What Is Technical Analysis?

The first place to start here is looking at what technical analysis is all about. This is a strategy that we can use in order to take a look at some of our investments, evaluate them a bit, and then find the best opportunities to help us jump into the market and trade for a profit. These are usually found by analyzing some of the statistical trends on particular security gathered from the trading activity, such as the price movement and the volume.

This basically means that we are going to use a lot of charts and graphs to help us make some decisions on what will happen with a particular security. We can look these over and determine whether the stock or security will go up or down, how far in either direction it will go, and whether we should purchase or sell based on those trends. It doesn't usually take into account any of the other factors about the company itself, assuming that the charts and graphs will tell us the information that we need.

Unlike what we see with a fundamental analysis, which we will explore in more detail in the next chapter, this analysis is going to try and focus on the price or the volume of the stock and see what will happen next. These tools of technical analysis are going to be used as a way to figure out what the supply and demand for the security are and how that is going to change the price. This gives us the implied volatility as well.

This seems like a lot, but by carefully exploring and studying the charts that we are able to find, it is possible to see how this works and when we should make our trades. The technical analysis is often a good option to use in order to generate some trading signals for the short-term from a lot of tools during charting. But we can also use it to help improve the evaluation that we do with the strength of the security, or even the weakness of the security, based on the broader market or one of the sectors that go with it. This is very valuable information because it helps us to improve our estimations.

The technical analysis can be used on any and every security that you want, as long as that security has some historical trading data to go with it. This means that we are able to complete this technical analysis on anything that we want, including currencies, commodities, stocks, and futures, to name a few. We will work with stocks because that is the option that most people like to use when they enter into the stock market, but it is not the only choice out there.

To recap, there are a few things that we need to remember before we dive into the rest of this chapter. This includes:

1. Technical analysis is basically going to be a discipline of trading that is used in order to do

an evaluation of investments and then identify some of the opportunities of trading based on the price patterns and trends that we are able to see while looking at the charts

2. The technical analyst will believe that the activity and some of the price changes of the past will be able to tell them all they need to know about where the security will go in the future.

3. We can see that this is different than the fundamental analysis because we focus more on the charts, rather than on the fundamentals of the company itself.

The Basics of Technical Analysis

Another thing that we need to take a look at here is some of the basics that come with this technical analysis. This was a theory that was introduced as the Dow Theory by Charles Dow during the late 1800s. there are a number of important researchers out there who helped to add to the concepts we see in this theory to make sure that we are able to get the basics of it, and can use it properly. Then in our modern world, the technical analysis has seen some changes so that it can include so many different signals and patterns, hundreds of them by some estimates, though lots of research.

This type of analysis is going to work based on the assumption that trading activity from the past, and the changes in price from the past, of a security, can be really valuable indicators of the future movements in the price of that security when it is paired together with some of the other tradings and investing worlds.

There are a lot of people who will use this kind of technical analysis. For example, professionals in this will use the technical analysis along with some other forms of research in order to get the best results and make the best decisions. Retail traders are going to sometimes make decisions that are based right on the price of the charts that they get with that security and some other statistics. But if you go through and do this for a long time, you will find that technical and fundamental analysis should not be used on their own.

The Assumptions of the Technical Analysis

There are going to be two methods that we can use when it is time to analyze the securities that we want to work with, and when we make some good investment decisions. These include the technical analysis that we are talking about here and the fundamental analysis.

As a brief overview, the fundamental analysis is going to be when we look at the financials of the business, and some of their potential in order to really determine the fair value that the business has. And then we can make some decisions based on that. Then there is a technical analysis, which is going to have us look at a lot of the charts that we want to focus on to make some decisions. This one will assume that the price that is found in the charts will already show all of the information that we need to know about the company, and we can then focus on some of the statistical analysis of the price movements to make these decisions.

When we work with the technical analysis, it is going to try and understand some of the sentiments of the market that are found behind the trends in the price of that security. This is going to be one that will look for patterns and trends instead of looking and analyzing the fundamental attributes of the security.

here are a few important things that we need to remember when it comes to working with the technical analysis, and knowing how to make this work is going to be so important to our overall success. Some of the things that we need to consider to get the most out of the technical analysis include:

1. The market already discounts everything

Those who follow this kind of analysis already believe that everything about the company, including market psychology, the various market factors that are out there, and some of the fundamentals of the company, are already reflected in the stock price. It assumes that we do not need to go through and do any more work than looking at the charts because this will tell us all that we need to know.

With this assumption in place, we just have one thing left to work on. We need to spend time analyzing the price movements, which we are going to be able to find inside some of the charts that we look through for that company. The technical analyst is going to look at this and see the price changes as the product of supply and demand for a certain stock that they are trying to look through on the market.

2. The price will move on trends

In addition to what we have taken a look at above, the technical analysis is going to expect that the prices that happen with the stock, even some of the market movements that are random are going to exhibit a trend that we can follow, no matter what kind of time frame we are looking at. This is good news because we are able to look at a particular stock and notice when it is going to head up and when it will go down and can make some smart decisions along the way.

The idea here is that the price of the stock, no matter what stock you are working with, is most likely to go on with a past trend rather than having it move erratically. There may be some exceptions for a short amount of time, but for the most part, the stock price is going to stick to the trend. Most technical trading strategies that you will want to work with are completely based on this assumption.

3. History is going to repeat

The third thing that we need to look at when it is time to work on technical analysis is that history is more likely to repeat itself. Technical analysts believe that history is going to repeat itself over and over again. The price movements that we can look at are repetitive in nature, and this is because of market psychology, which is actually more predictable than we may think. It is often going to be based on the emotions of people, like fear and excitement. When people are excited about a stock, they are more likely to purchase it. When they are scared about the price dropping or something happening on the stock, then they will sell.

The technical analysis is going to work with chart patterns to help analyze these emotions and then the market movements that come with it, to make sure they can learn more about the trends that may show up. While there are a lot of forms that come with technical analysis and why this method has been around for over 100 years, they are still really relevant because they are good at showing us some patterns that come in the price movements, and since they repeat themselves, it is a good thing to look at.

How to Use the Technical Analysis

This kind of analysis will work on forecasting some of the movements in the price of any security that you can work with, and it is often going to be subject to the forces of demand and supply. In fact, there are some who see this as a process that helps them to see the supply and demand forces based on the movements in the market price of that security. Often this is something that will apply back to the changes in prices, but some analysts are more likely to track some other numbers along the way than the price, including the open interest figures, and trading volume if they needed to.

When you look through any industry, there will be hundreds of signals and patterns, and researchers are always developing some more to help support the trading that uses this. The technical analysts will work with more than one type of trading system in order to make it easier to forecast and trade on these movements in price.

Some of the indicators that we can use will be focused on identifying the current trend in the market, including some of the resistance and support areas, while others are going to be focused more on figuring out how strong a trend is and how likely it is that the trend will continue into the future. There are a lot of technical indicators that we are able to focus on, along with some good charting patterns that we can add in, and these include options like the moving averages, channels, trendlines, and momentum indicators.

To keep it simple, a technical analyst will take a look at a lot of indicators to help them out, and some of the ones that you will get really familiar with as we go through this process include:

1. The price trends
2. Support and resistance levels
3. Chart patterns
4. Moving averages
5. Oscillators

6. Momentum and volume indicators

These are just a few of the options that we are able to work with based on how the market is going, how your stock is behaving, and even based on what seems to work the best for your needs. You may want to try out a few of these to figure out which ones seem to give you the best results when you trade and work from there.

Some Limitations That Come With Technical Analysis

There are a lot of options that come with using the technical analysis, and this is one of the best options to make sure that we can get some profits when we work on swing trading. But this is not the option that you will want to use all of the time. There are a few limitations that show up when we want to work with this type of analysis.

Some researchers and analysts worry that this is not going to work the way that we would like when it is time to start investing. The EMH will show us why we should not expect any kind of actionable information inside the price and volume data in the past of the stock. However, with this same kind of reasoning, business fundamentals should not provide any kind of information that we can act on either. These points of view are going to be referred back to the weak form and the semi-strong form of the EMH.

Another issue that can show up when we use the technical analysis is that history is never going to repeat itself the exact same way all the time. This means that the price patter study that we do with the technical analysis is kind of dubious and may not provide the results that we are hoping for. It is often better to see the prices modeled by assuming a random walk. Whether you think that history will repeat itself will make a big difference in whether you will actually use this method or not.

Then there is also a third criticism that shows up with this as well. this one talks about how the technical analysis can work in some instances, but only because it fulfills the self-fulfilling prophecy. For example, the technical trader is going to place a stop-loss order below what is the 200-day moving average of a certain company. If there are a lot of traders who have done the same thing and then the stock does go to this point, there will all of a sudden be a huge number of orders to sell things, and that will push the price of the stock back down. This basically just confirms the movement that the traders were anticipating in the first place.

Then, there are other traders who will see some of these price decreases and then work on selling the position they have, which is going to be there to reinforce the strength of the trend that we see. This type of short-term selling pressure is kind of the same idea, but it is not going to have much bearing on where the price of the asset will be in a few weeks or even a few months from now.

Basically, if there are enough traders in the market who use the same signals,then it is possible that they will have the right amount of pressure to cause the movement they were working with through the signal. But over the long-term, this group will not be enough to drive the price and this will not work out as well for them as they had hoped.

Is the Technical Analysis of a Good Strategy?

There are a lot of good reasons to use the technical analysis, but there are also a lot of researchers and analysts who advise not to use it at all this can make it confusing to someone who is new to this and who would wonder whether it is actually going to help them to see some results with trading.

There are a ton of swing traders who work with this kind of strategy. It is easy to work with and allows us to work with some of the trends and the charts that go with the stock or another security that we want to use. And that is all that you need to focus on. And since you are not planning on keeping this position for the long-term, and your goals are to sell it off within a few weeks, often the fundamentals are not that important, and you will get all of the information you need from the trade from your charts and graphs.

For some of the most successful swing traders, using a combination of the technical and the fundamental analysis will be the best way to make sure that you are successful with your trades. This allows you to learn more about what works best with the trends of the company and how their prices have gone up and down while also taking a look at how the company is doing financially and looking at some of the news that surrounds it as well before making your decisions.

Combining the technical and the fundamental analysis is one of the best ways to make sure that you get the full picture of a stock and the company that controls it as well. And the more information that you have about that company and about that stock, the easier it can be to make predictions on where the price will move in the future, and whether this is a good option to help you be successful and take home a profit.

The technical analysis is a pretty easy strategy to understand. You will take a look at a lot of the charts and graphs that come with the stock or the security that you want to work on, and then you make some decisions on where the price of the stock will go in the future. Sometimes we add in fundamental analysis, or at least pay some attention to the news, to figure out if there will be some big spikes, either up or down, that may not show up in the charts and other research that we do.

The idea with the technical analysis is that we will focus more on the price movements and the idea of supply and demand. Many professional traders will use more than one method to make sure they pick the right stocks, and you can too. Later on, we will look at a few of the strategies that we can utilize that are all considered technical analysis tools, and that will help us to know what signs and signals we need to look at before making some of our purchasing decisions.

CHAPTER 4

HOW THE FUNDAMENTAL ANALYSIS IS DIFFERENT

Once we have had some time to learn more about the technical analysis and how that will work, it is time for us to move on to learn more about the fundamental analysis and how we can use this for our needs. This option is not going to spend as much time looking at the charts and graphs that come with some of the stocks and securities that we want to use. It may glance at them a bit, but it focuses more on some of the options that will help to determine whether the company that is under the stock, is secure and has some good things behind it. then the analyst will determine whether the current price of the stock is undervalued or overvalued based on that information.

There are a lot of parts that have to come together in order to work on the fundamental analysis. And many will agree that using this method is a lot more in-depth and harder to work on compared to the technical analysis that we talked about before. This should not deter you at all because it is a great strategy that can help you get good deals on some of the stocks or securities that you want to use. It is just a little bit different. Let's dive in and look at how we can use this.

What Is Fundamental Analysis?

The first thing that we need to take a look at here is the fundamental analysis. This is going to be a method that a trader is able to use in order to measure out the intrinsic value of security because we will examine some of the different factors that we can see that may influence the price of the stock, including the financial and the economic factors.

A fundamental analyst will study anything that is able to affect the value of the security, including some of the macroeconomic factors like how the economy is doing and some of the conditions of the particular industry you are focusing on, all the way to some of the microeconomic factors, like how effective the management of the company can be.

The end goal of doing this is to come up with a number that the investor is going to use for what they think the price of the security should be. They can then take that and compare it to the current price of that security to figure out whether the security is undervalued or overvalued. This makes it easier to figure out whether the trader should dive in and purchase the security or not.

This is a method of analyzing a stock or another security, and it works in contrast to the technical analysis that we were talking about in the previous chapter. This one looks more at the daily running around the business, and some of the outside factors that can influence the business, rather than worrying about the historical data and how the price will move based on these trends.

There are a few points that we can keep in mind here to make sure that we understand how this is supposed to work and how we can ensure that we get the best results will include the following:

1. This kind of analysis is going to be the method that we can use to figure out the fair market value of a stock and then decide whether the current price is above or under that.
2. The trader who uses this option will search around for some stocks that are currently trading at prices that are lower or higher than what their real value is all about.

3. If the fair market value is higher than what the price of the market is, then this shows us that the stock is being undervalued in the market right now. It is recommended to purchase the stock when this happens because it is likely that the market will go up, and we can make some profit in the process.

Understanding How the Fundamental Analysis Works

Now we need to take a closer look at how the fundamental analysis can be used for some of your trading needs. All analysis of the stock market will try to figure out whether the value of a security is valued well or not within the whole market. Fundamental analysis will often be done from the macro to the micro perspective so that we can better find some of the securities that are not being priced well, or the right way, in the market.

Analysts who use this option are going to study many different things to figure this out, including how the economy is working and doing, and then the strength of the industry that the specific security is in right then. When this is all done, the trader will move on to looking at the performance of that individual company and how it compares to some of the other companies in the industry. This helps them to arrive at the market value that is fair for that stock.

This kind of analysis is going to make use of lots of public data to help evaluate the value of the stock or any other security that you want to work with. For example, it is common for an investor can perform fundamental analysis on the value of the bond, and they will do it by looking at the economic factors that are out there, including some of the interest rates available, and then how the state of the economy is behaving at the time. Then we are able to study the information about the bond issuer, including some changes that may show up in the credit rating of the company.

For stocks, fundamental analysis is going to look at a lot of different things to figure out the value of the company and how much potential that is there for the company to grow in the future. For example, we would want to look at things like the profit margins, the return on equity, the future growth, earnings, and revenues, along with a few other options, to figure all of this out. The good news is that while there are a lot of options out there that we need to explore and look at, all of this data is available in the financial statements that the company has to release to the public so you can get it easily.

Fundamental Analysis and Investing

There are a lot of times when the fundamental analysis is going to be used in investing, especially in the stock market. In this one, the trader will take some time to create their own model to determine the value of the company based on the data that is publicly out there for them. The value they come up with is only an estimate, and the opinion of the trader, of what the price of the company's shares should be. Then they can compare it to the price that the shares are currently trading out. Some analysts could call this estimated price the intrinsic value of the company.

If a trader comes in and finds that the stock's value should be significantly higher than the current price of the market of the stock, then they may publish a buy rating for the stock. This is going to be the recommendation to investors who follow that analyst. If the trader then goes through and sees things the opposite way and find a lower intrinsic value than the current price of the market, the stock is considered overvalued, and then they will issue out a recommendation to sell.

Investors who decide to follow some of these recommendations will expect that they would then be able to buy stocks that are favorable, and that will provide them with some profitability as well. Many times beginners are going to look at what the analysts say and follow all that, but it is possible to go through and do the analysis on your own and come to your own conclusions as well.

The Difference Between Qualitative and Quantitative Fundamental Analysis

One of the problems that will come with defining the word fundamentals is that it is possible that it will cover anything and everything that will relate back to the well-being economically of the company. They will include some obvious numbers like the profits and the revenue of the company, but it is possible that it can include a lot of other things, like the quality of the management of this company and the market share as well.

The good news here is that there are a lot of fundamental factors that we can include, but we are able to group them into two broad categories to make it easier to understand what is going on here. And these two categories are going to include qualitative and quantitative options. The financial meaning that we see with the terms is going to be similar to their standard definitions, but to review, the definitions that we will use include:

1. Quantitative: This means that the item is capable of being expressed or measured in numerical terms.
2. Qualitative: This is something that is based or related to the quality of the character of something, rather than the quantity or the size of it.

With this as our context, the quantitative fundamentals that we will want to use are more about the hard numbers. These are going to be some of the characteristics that we can measure the business. This is why we will see the biggest sources of this data type will be in the financial statements. You can also go through and look at the assets, profits, and revenue and get the measurements with great precision.

Then we can look at some of the qualitative fundamentals, which are considered less tangible through this. They could include things like the quality of the top executives of the company, the recognition of the brand name, the patents, and more. These are a bit harder to look through when we focus on the company, but they are still important and have some value that we need to look at.

We need to consider here that neither of the two fundamentals is not going to be seen as more important than the other one. In fact, most people who work with these will consider both of them at the same time to make some of their decisions. Let's take a look at some of the factors that we can consider with both of these and learn how this can be beneficial to our needs.

The Qualitative Fundamentals

There are a lot of things that we can consider when we are working through all of this and figuring out the qualitative fundamentals along the way. There are four main fundamentals that we will want to take a look at when we focus on the qualitative fundamentals, and these include:

The model of the business. With this one, we are going to spend some time looking at what the company does. This can be harder to pin down than it seems something. If there is a company that will sell fast-food chicken, is it making its money that way, or is it working on royalties and some fees from franchisees? These are things that we need to consider before we make our decisions.

Then we can look at some of the competitive advantages that we are able to work with on that company. The long-term success that a company has is driven quite a bit by how well it can be competitive in the industry, and how they can keep this edge. The more powerful this advantage, the safer the business is, and it can keep others at bay while the company will enjoy some profits and growth in the process. When a company is able to add on some of this kind of competitive advantage, then the shareholders are going to do well and can see some good profits for years to come.

Another thing that we need to take a look at its management. Some believe that this is actually the most important thing that we need to consider when investing in the company. This makes a lot of sense if we think it through. Even some of the best models in business will be doomed if the people who run and lead the company do not execute the plan well or don't take care of the company.

Of course, as someone who is simply investing in the company, it is hard to go in and meet and see how the managers are doing, you can still take a look at the corporate website, check out the resumes of those who are in charge, and read the news to see what is going on with the company. This can help you to take a look at how the management is doing and whether they will continue to do the great work that you need in the future.

And the fourth thing that we are going to take a look at is something known as corporate governance. This will include all of the policies that are found in the company that will tell us more about the responsibilities and the relationships between the stakeholders, the directors, and the management. These policies are going to be determined and defined right from the company charter and some of their bylaws, along with some of the corporate laws and regulations that they need to focus on.

You want to do business and do some of the tradings with a company that is run in an ethical manner, one that is fair, transparent, and as efficient as possible. If any of these are gone, then you could be in trouble when you try to invest. You should take some particular note of whether the management respects the rights of the shareholders and their interests as well. check to see whether the communication they have with the shareholders is understandable, clear, and transparent. If you do not get what is being said, there is usually a good reason for this, and that can be a big red flag along the way.

The final thing that we are going to work with this one is the industry that the company is in. you can also look at information like the business cycles, regulation, competition, the growth of the whole industry, the market share among all the firms in the industry, and the customer base. Learning about the whole industry and then comparing it back to the company you want to invest in can make it easier to see the financial health of the company.

The Quantitative Fundamentals

Since we have had some time to look more at some of the qualitative fundamentals, we need to look at some more of the quantitative options as well. these are going to focus a bit more on some of the financials that are found with the company to make sure that it is steady and secure. You don't want to get into an investment and then find out that the company just filed bankruptcy, and your investment is gone.

This one will work a lot with the financial statements of the company. These statements are going to be the medium used by a company to show all the information that investors, current and potential, will need about its financial performance. Followers of this kind of analysis will take a look at this data and use it to make some of the investment decisions.

There are a number of financial statements and more that we can look at depending on the strategy that we want to use. The three that you should definitely take some time on and explore, no matter what other strategies you work on, include the cash flow statements, the balance sheets, and the income statements.

First on the list is the balance sheet. This is an important financial statement of a company that will take a look at all the equity, liabilities, and assets of a company at one particular point in time. These three things will change on a regular basis, so that is why we must remember that it is up to date based on when the report was generated. The balance sheet is going to be named this way because it will have the financial structure balances of the company listed out with the following formula:

Assets = Liabilities + Shareholders/Equity

The assets are going to show us all the resources that the business is in control over or owns at that particular period of time. This can include many things like buildings, machinery, inventory, and cash. These are important to help us see how well the company is doing overall.

Then we can move over to the other part of the equation. This is going to show us the total of the value of the financing the company may be using, and that is still owed, in order to get those assets. Financing is going to come as a result of equity or liabilities. Liabilities are going to represent the debt, which the company has to pay back at some point, and then the equity is going to show the total value of money that the owners have already added back to the business. This equity can include the retained earnings or the profit that was made in the previous years.

This is an important thing to look through. While it is not a bad thing for a company to have some debt in order to purchase the machinery and the other items that they need, it can get out of hand. If the debts are too high and it seems like the company is drowning and not going to be able to pay back those debts, then this is a red flag that should keep you away from investing in them.

Once we are all done with the balance sheet, we are able to move on to what is known as the income statement. While the balance sheet is a good snapshot to tell us a lot about the finances of the business, the income statement is going to measure the performance of the company over a time frame. So, the balance sheet is usually over a month or a day, and then the income statement is going to be moreover a quarter or a whole year so you can see how they handle their finances and more throughout the time.

The income statement is a good option to take a look at along the way, and you should not focus on the fundamental analysis without looking at this. You will find that it is going to present you with a lot of information about the profits, expenses, and revenues that the company was able to generate over a certain time period by doing their normal business operations.

And the final of the three financial statements that you need to take a look at to complete your fundamentals analysis here is the statement of cash flows. This is going to be a record that we can look over to see the cash inflows and outflows of business over some period of time. This is usually going to look at a few important cash related activities, including:

1. The operating cash flow: This is the cash the business is able to generate from their daily business operations.

2. Cash from financing: This is going to be all the cash that is received or paid from issuing and borrowing funds.

3. Cash from investing: This is going to be the cash that would be used to invest in assets, and sometimes it is the proceeds from the sale of other long-term assets, equipment, and businesses.

This statement is an important one to spend some time on because it is really hard for a business to go in and manipulate at all. There are a lot of accountants who can become aggressive here and manipulate the earnings hat they have, but it is tough to fake cash in the bank. For this reason, this is going to be a good conservative measure that we are able to look at to see more about the performance of the company.

The Idea of Intrinsic Value

One of the primary assumptions that we can make when it comes to working with the fundamental analysis is that the current price that we can see for the stock on the stock market is not really telling us much about the company and what it is really worth. A second assumption that will come up is that the valet hat we get from the fundamental data of the company is going to help us to see the true value of the stock, and then we can make some better choices based on that.

It is common for analysts to refer to this hypothetical true value as something known as the intrinsic value. However, we have to note that using the phrase of intrinsic value means something different when we work with stock valuation than it will mean with other choices like options trading. When we talk about options trading, we are going to work with a standard calculation to figure out our intrinsic value. For the stock market, we would use a variety of complex models to get the intrinsic value of the stock. There is not a single formula that is accepted and used all over for how to find this intrinsic value.

For example, let's say that we find a stock for one company that is trading at $20. We do some of the research that is required for fundamental analysis and determine that the stock should be worth at least $24. Then there is another analyst who comes in and thinks that the value of that same stock should be closer to $26. Many investors here would consider the average of the estimates and then assume that the value is closer to $25 based on this. Often the investor would see these as relevant estimates because they want to purchase stocks that are trading at prices that are significantly below some of these intrinsic values.

We can take this the other way as well. If you find that there is a stock listed out at $20, but your research and your own fundamental analysis says that it is worth $15, then this is not a good one to go with. If the market catches up with it, then the price of the stock will go down, and you would lose money if you purchased at the $20 mark.

This will lead us to the third assumption that we need to make about the fundamental analysis. With this one, in the long run, the stock market is going to always meet up with the fundamentals. It may take some time, and we don't really know how long that can be, whether it is days or years or some other time frame, but at some point, this will happen.

And that is what the fundamental analysis is all about. When we are able to focus on a particular business, then we are able to estimate the intrinsic value of a firm and find all of the opportunities to purchase that at a discount. The investment is going to pay off sometime in the future when the market finally catches up with those fundamentals.

Criticisms of This Method

While we are here, we need to take a look at some of the criticisms that come with this analysis. One of the main criticisms that we will see with this kind of analysis will come with two groups of things; the proponents who want to work with the technical analysis, and then those who believe in the efficient market hypothesis.

First, we will dive into those who like to work with the technical analysis. This is the other method that we talked about, one that relies heavily on all of the charts and the graphs that you are able to find, and then you make your decisions based on that. Since the fundamental analysis isn't going to spend as much time on the charts and graphs, these are really different options to work with.

One of the basic ideas that come with this technical analysis is that the stock market is already going to take into account all of the fundamentals and that it discounts everything. All the news that is publicly available to us about the company will be reflected in the price of the stock. This is why the fundamental analysis would not work, according to these traders. The price movements of the stock, in their opinion, will provide us with more insight compared to looking at the underlying fundamentals.

Then we need to look a bit more at something known as the efficient market hypothesis. Followers of this are usually going to be in some kind of disagreement with both of the analysis types that we have talked about. This may sound confusing, but they take a different approach to look at the market and figuring out what works and what does not.

This hypothesis is going to state that it is pretty much impossible to beat out the market through technical analysis or the fundamental analysis. Since the market has already priced out the stocks as efficiently as possible, and it does this on an ongoing basis, any opportunities for excess returns are going to be whittled away by all of the participants in the market. This means that it is almost impossible for anyone to really outperform the market when it comes to working with it over the long term.

All of these methods have their merits, and it really depends on what we are trying to accomplish and what or end goals are all about. When we are able to look through the documents and the financial statements of a company, we can sometimes find some hidden gems that will tell us more about the process and all that it entails as well. but sometimes, this is not going to provide us with the right information and technical analysis, with us pouring over charts and learning about the markets that way will be the right method.

Often combining the two of these together will be the right answer and can provide us with a good way to figure out which stocks we want to work with overall. This can make life a bit easier to work with this method, but you have to choose which one is the best for your needs as well. both can be efficient for swing trading, so go with the one that makes the most sense for you.

CHAPTER 5

SWING TRADING WITH DIFFERENT SECURITIES

Before we go into some of the basics of the strategies that we are able to work with as we go through this process, we need to make sure that we understand some of the different securities that you can use when it is time to start swing trading. You can technically work with any kind of security that you would like when it is time to start swing trading, though we did spend quite a bit of time looking at how to do this with stocks because that is the most common option. Let's take a look at a few of the other choices that you can make when it is time to start trading with the various securities that are available for you.

Swing Trading With Stocks

The first option that we can take a look at is the stocks. This is the most common instrument to use when we want to trade, especially with swing trading, because it is the least complicated choice out there. But we need to take a look at this a bit more. First, what is a stock? This is basically a security that will help to show what percentage of ownership you have in a company. And it will entitle the owner of the stock a proportion of the assets and profits of the corporation. This is equal to how much stock you own. These units will be known as shares.

The stocks are going to be purchased and then sold on the stock exchanges, though there are times when a private sale can happen, and we will find these stocks are the foundation of the portfolio for most people. These transactions do have to meet up with some regulations from the government to ensure that an investor is protected from those who try to defraud them. You can also purchase them from most of the online stock brokers who are out there.

So, how do you get one of these stocks? It is common for companies to issue, or sell, stocks to help them to raise funds to operate their business. The holder of the stock, which would be you if you purchase one during swing trading, has basically purchased a piece of the corporation, and, depending on what kind of shares they hold onto, they could also have some kind of claim on the earnings and assets of the company.

What this means is that the shareholder is technically an owner of that company, along with others who own the stock as well. ownership is going to be based on how many of these shares you own relative to how many outstanding shares you have. Those who have 10,000 shares would have a higher ownership in the company compared to those who have 100 shares, for example.

Keep in mind with this one, that you do not actually own the company. You will own the shares that the company issues. But the corporation is a special thing, and by law, they are treated as legal persons. This means that they are able to file taxes, can borrow, can own some property, and can be sued just like a regular person. The idea that the corporations that are out there are a person means that it is able to own their own assets. So all of the chairs and equipment and computers in the company will belong to it and not to its shareholders.

This is an important distinction because it shows us hat the company is separated legally from the property of the shareholders, which helps to limit how much liability of the company and the shareholder, so that is a good thing for you as well. for example, if the company goes bankrupt, a judge can order all of the assets to be sold, but you will never have your assets taken from you if something goes wrong with the company.

As a swing trader, you will not hold onto the stocks for very long. But it is still important to understand some of the basics that go with this and what the stocks mean if you are using them for trading and other purposes. They are easy to purchase and sell during normal business hours on the stock exchange, which can make them an attractive choice if you are working as a swing trader.

Swing Trading With Options

Another choice that we can make when we want to work with swing trading is something known as options trading. These are slightly different than the stock market, though there are a few parts that you will recognize as your work with this. To start, options are going to be financial instruments that are derivatives that are then based on the value of the underlying securities, including stocks and other options.

The options will offer the buyer the opportunity to sell or purchase, based on the type of contract that you hold onto, the underlying asset. Unlike what we can do with the futures, the person who has the contract does not have to sell or buy that asset if they choose not to. There are two types of options that we are able to work with as well. The first choice that you have the call options will allow the holder to purchase the asset at a stated price within a specific timeframe. The put options will allow the holder to sell the asset at a stated price within a specific timeframe.

Both of those contracts will have an expiration date by which the holder will be able to exercise that option if they would like. The price that is stated on the option is called the strike price, and it is common that these options will be sold and bought through retail or online brokers in most cases.

That was an introduction to what options are about, but how should we work with these options if we choose to use this for swing trading? Options are a really versatile financial product to work with. The contracts are going to involve a buyer and a seller. The buyer will come in and pay an options premium for the rights that are granted through the contract. Each call option will have a bullish buyer in them, and then the seller will be bearish. The put options will be the opposite of a bullish seller and a bearish buyer.

We will find that the options contracts will usually represent about 100 shares of the security that is under it, and then the buyer is able to pay a premium fee for each contract they want to work with. So, if you have an option that has the premium set to 35 cents for each control, if you purchased one of these options, which is 100 shares, it would cost you $35. Keep in mind that this is a really oversimplified method to work with, and it is likely that you will need to pay more than this to get things going.

The premium is something that all buyers will have to pay in order to get this started, and the amount that you pay is based on the strike price. Remember that the strike price is the price you pay for buying or selling the security until that expiration date that is set up on it. Another factor in the premium price that you will pay is the expiration date. If that date is close, then the price will be a bit lower, but if there is a lot of time for the underlying asset to make a move, then the price will be lower.

Traders and investors will be able to come in and choose whether to purchase or sell these options any time that they would like. And they may choose the options as their vehicle for investing for a number of reasons. First, speculating on these options will allow you to come in and hold a leveraged position on an asset at a lower cost compared to purchasing the direct shares of that asset. The investor will also have the choice to hedge or reduce some of the exposure that comes with their portfolio when they use this. And then, there are some situations where the option holder is able to generate income when they use these call options or work as an options writer.

The reason that people will choose to go with options is going to vary based on some of their own goals and what they hope to get out of the market in the process. You can choose to use this because it is seen as safer, the costs of joining are lower, and it can be a lot of fun. And it does work well with some of the swing tradings we have been talking about, so that is a great choice.

One thing that we need to discuss before we leave here and move on to some of the other choices you can make for swing trading is the idea that there are two types of options; the American options and the European options. The American options are the ones that you can exercise any time before the expiration date on the option. On the other hand, the European options are the ones that you have to hold onto until the expiration date, and then you can use them.

Swing Trading With Forex

Stocks and options are the two most likely choices that beginners with swing trading are going to make to help them get into the market and enjoy the results with some good profits. But there are other choices that can really open up some more doors to what you can do and can make the trading a bit more interesting in the process. In this section, we will take a bit of time to look at forex trading and how well this can work with some of your needs as a swing trader.

Forex is basically a trading method of foreign currency and exchange. It is the process of taking one currency and changing it over to another currency for a variety of reasons. If you have ever traveled to another country and used their money, or purchased something and had it shipped to you from Europe, then you have participated in the Forex market at some point. We can even use this as one of the methods to help us trade and get amazing results.

This is a really large market, which can be intimidating for someone who is just entering it and trying to find their way. according to a recent report that the Bank for International Settlements released, it is estimated that the Forex market has a trading volume of more than $5.1 trillion a day. That is an extraordinary amount.

To help us see whether this is the right investment vehicle for our needs, we need to look more at what the forex market entails. This is basically a market where we will exchange various types of currencies. Currencies are so important to many people around the world, even if you do not realize it at first. This is because we use currencies to help conduct some of the foreign trade and the business we want to accomplish.

We use it on a daily basis, even if we are not trading on the forex market.

Let's say that you are living in the United States and choose to purchase a designer dress, or some other product from France, who relies on Euros while you rely on the USD. You or the company you purchase the dress from has to pay the French for the dress in Euros. And that means we need to bring into the game a U.S. importer who could help to exchange these and make sure that the person in France who made the dress is getting paid the right amount.

This is the same when we want to travel. We can come from any country in the world, but if we head to Egypt to take a look at some of the pyramids that are out there, then we need to make sure that we bring in the right currency, or we are out of luck. This is the most common way that we think about the forex market, as a way for us to exchange our money to go traveling and get it in the right currency for the area that we want to visit.

But there are a lot of options that we can use for this one, including spending our time investing in the market and exchanging one currency for another to make as much money as possible. This one is a bit more difficult because you have to know a lot about your own country of origin, as well as the country you would like to switch with. This is a bit more complicated since there are two variables, and you need to know the relations that happen between both.

But if you do it well, it can help you make some good money.

One thing that is really unique about this kind of international market is that there isn't really a central marketplace for it like we see with stocks and options. Rather, currency trading is something that is done electronically and through a method known as over the counter. What this means for us is that all of the transactions happen between the traders in all parts of the world thanks to a vast computer network, rather than relying on one centralized exchange.

Another neat thing that you will notice with this one is that the market is open five and a half days a week and for 24 hours during those days, without a stop. This also allows us to trade all of the major currencies throughout the world, and you can use this in any of the major financial centers of the world. This means that even if the trading times end in the United States, you can then start it all anew in another market that is just opening. This can allow for a lot of activity no matter what time of day you decide to do your work.

This is a really unique way of handling some of the swing tradings that you would like to do, and it will bring in some new challenges that are a lot of fun. You have to consider how much risk you are willing to take, and whether or not you are able to keep up with the demand and all of the research that is necessary to do this for two currencies in comparison with one another. But for those who can do so successfully, the forex market can be a great place to do some trading.

Swing Trading With Futures

The final choice that we will take a look at when it is time to do some swing trading is known as futures. Futures are going to be kind of similar to what we see with options, but with a few slight differences, that will be important if you decide to work with them. To start, these futures are basically going to be a derivative financial contract that will obligate those in the party to transact an asset at a predetermined future date and price. Here the buyer must purchase, or the seller has to sell the underlying asset at the set price, regardless of the current market price when the expiration date gets there.

With options, you can buy or sell, based on the contract, any time before the expiration date if you would like. And if things go south and don't work well for you, you can walk away and agree not to do anything with the contract. With the future, this is not true. You have to work with the contract and complete the right actions when the expiration date happens.

There are also a number of underlying assets that you can use here, including physical commodities and some other financial instruments that are wide open here as well. The contracts that come up here will show us how much of the underlying asset we work with, and they can be standardized in a way to make sure that we can trade well and easily on this kind of exchange as well.

Futures can also be known as futures contracts, and they allow the trader to lock in the price of the commodity or the underlying asset if they choose. These contracts will come to us with some expiration dates and a set price that will be known from the start. Futures are going to be known based on when they expire. For example, a December Gold futures contract will be done in December. The term here is going to help show the overall market in most cases. However, there are also a lot of types of these contracts that you can choose from including:

1. Commodity futures. These would include options like wheat, corn, natural gas, and crude oil.

2. Stock index futures like the S&P 500 index.

3. Precious metals that would include silver and gold

4. Currency futures including those for the USD< Euro, and the British pound.

5. Any U.S. Treasury futures for bonds and a few other products as well.

As we mentioned before, there are a few differences between futures and options, so we need to know how these are the same and different, so we need to consider that before choosing either. However, even with some of the issues and restrictions that come with this, there are a lot of benefits that come with it, including:

1. Investors are able to use these kinds of contracts to help them speculate on the direction in the price of an asset that is underlying their contract.
2. Companies are able to hedge the price of their raw materials or products that they already sell from some bad movements in the price.
3. These contracts may only require us to come up with a fraction of the contract amount, or a deposit, with the broker before we can get into the game.

There are some risks to working with this, of course. It is possible that you can go into this and lose more than the initial amount that you put down since futures will work with lots of leverage. Investing in a futures contract can cause a company that is hedged to miss out on some of the price movements that are more favorable. And then there is the idea of margin. This is a great thing in some cases but can be bad in others. It means that all of your gains are amplified, but your losses will be as well.

As we can see, there are a lot of choices that we are able to choose from when we wan to get started with swing trading. And all of them can provide us with some amazing benefits and can be a great way to make some money in the process. Do your research and figure out which one is the best for your needs.

CHAPTER 6

THE SWING TRADING STRATEGIES TO HELP YOU WIN

Now that we have had a lot of time to look at what swing trading is all about and how great it can be to work with this method of investing, it is time to take this a little bit further and look more at some of the strategies that we can use to really take our swing trading and make it as effective as possible. These strategies can all work in certain types of trades, and it depends on what you are the most comfortable with and how the market is behaving. Learning at least a few of them and gaining some confidence when using them will make a world of difference in how well you can make this happen. Let's dive in and look at some of the best options that you can go with when it is time to start swing trading

The Hull Moving Average Strategy

This is going to be a method that you can use that is completely based on the hull moving average indicator. If you have never heard about this, it is a moving average indicator that is smooth and will move really fast. This is going to be a good thing because it is able to eliminate any of the lag that shows up in your work and can improve the smoothing all at the same time. What this means for us is that it is reactive to the price action as we go through with this.

There are two main ways that we are able to use this hull moving average to help us to purchase or sell something in the market. Some of these include:

1. We can look at the change of the slope. When this happens, then we know that it is time to get ready to purchase or sell our security.

2. If we see that the slope is going up, then it is time to purchase you can enter right then with the market order, or you can place your own buy stop pending order that is a few pips above the high of that new candlestick that should start to form and will cause your slow to go up. Make sure that this happens after the candlestick has time to close up.

3. If you see that the other slope is happening and it starts to go down, then it is time to prepare yourself to sell. You can either do this with a sell market order, or you can place your own sell stop pending order, as long as you do this somewhere between one to two pips under the low of your candlestick that is causing the slope of your hull to point down.

That is just one of the methods that you are able to use. It is also possible to work with something known as the Hull Moving Average Crossovers or the HMA. This one is going to be a fairly typical situation with a few of the other moving averages so you can check your work if you need it. Some of the steps that we can take to work with this method includes:

1. If you see that the faster HMA crosses the slower one to the upside, then this is a good sign that you are working with an uptrend.
2. If the faster HMA is able to cross the slower own going down, then this is a good sign that we are in a downtrend.
3. So what we want to do is wait around a bit for some of these HMA crossovers to happen, and then it is time to enter our buy or our sell order
4. If we are working with the setup to buy, we can either enter our own market order to place our own buy stop order. If we do this on our own, then it has to be done about one to two pips above the high candlestick that forms and will confirm the crossover. You can then place the stop loss in here as well, which will need to be around 5 pips below the low that you want.
5. For a sell setup, we are going to take the steps above and pretty much turn them around a bit to get our results. You would first enter into a sell market order, or you can do it yourself and work with a sell stop order hat is about one to

two pips below the low of your candlestick that will confirm the crossover. Then it is time to take that stop loss and place it about five pips above the high that comes with your candlestick.

And that is all that you need to work in order to make this strategy work. If you already know how to work with some of the basics of reading graphs and understanding what they say, then you will be set to go when it is time to work on this one as well. it is as simple as that and can work whether the market is going up or down, ensuring that you can keep on swing trading and getting the best results.

The ABCD Pattern

Another option that is really nice if you are into swing trading as a beginner is the ABCD pattern. This one is going to start us off with an upward move that is really strong. When this happens, you have a lot of buyers who are aggressively purchasing stock from point A, and then they will constantly bring in some new highs for that day, which will be point B. it is important to try and get in at B and trade here. But you do not want to chase the trade at all because B is usually higher than what the price is in the first place. Plus, this point is at a part where it is hard to know where to place the stop loss, and you do not want to get into a trade without this.

When you see that Point B shows up, the traders who have already gone in and purchased the stock at point A that we talked about earlier, will then start to sell off their stocks. This will not all happen at once, but it will slowly happen as a few decide to take the profits and call it good. This is not the time where you should enter the trade because it is hard to know when and where that pullback is going to happen.

If you are able to see that there is a bottom to this and the price just doesn't seem to go any further than it, then this is your point C. The security has found its support level, and you can go in and start planning the trade that you would like to use. If you get in at the right time and plan all of this out well, then you should be able to make a good amount of profit in the process.

This is a simple strategy that we are able to work with, which is why we are introducing it to you as a beginner. It is easy to understand and follow, and you won't feel as lost and confused along the way as some others may when they work on this one. There are a number of steps that we will have to use when we want to see this one work, and some of the steps will include:

- When you take a look through the scanner that you have set up, and you are looking for a stock, you want to look for one that is going o surge up from its original point A. You want it to get to a new high for that day. This is going to be point B.

- When these forms, you need to start paying attention. If you see that the new price is then going to become the support, and it goes up even more from there, then that is going to be point C. Be careful when you take a look at this because you have to wait for the right signs, rather than making assumptions and entering the market too soon.

- After you see the Point C showing up, you need to watch the stock carefully through this kind of consolidation period. From the information that you are able to gather at this time, you can then choose the right share size that you are comfortable with trading. You also need to spend this time looking for the stop and exit strategy that you would like to work with.

- When you see that the price is holding onto that support at point C, you should enter a trade at a point that is on or close to point C. The goal here is that your chosen security is going to move up to a new support point, known as point D, if not even higher.

- To work with this strategy, you want to have the stop loss end up at point C. If there is any time of the day where the price goes lower than your set point C, then you need to sell your stock and accept any losses that occur. The closer you can purchase the stock to that point C, the better with this strategy so that you can make sure your losses aren't too high.

- If you see that this stock continues to go higher, you will want to sell about half the position when it gets to point D. You can then move your stop higher to your entry point to help you make a profit.
- As soon as you see that the target is hit, or you see that the price is losing steam, even if it doesn't reach the goal, then you should sell the remaining shares that you have. When the price gets to a new low, this shows that the buyers are exhausted, and the trend will go backward.

There are a few steps that we need to follow to make this one work for our needs, but it is still a relatively simple process that even you as a beginner will be able to use and follow. However, to make it work as effectively as you would like, and to make sure that you can earn some profits from it, then you must have some patience. It is important with this one to only enter the markets at the right times, and to not get overly excited here, or you will end up losing a lot of money in the process.

Of course, we have to use some other caution here and be careful while watching the stock while you are in the trade, or you could miss out on a few things and lose a lot of money. It is possible that this trend can turn on you and start to go in a different direction than what you were planning, which is going to make it more difficult to work with and can cut into some of the profits that you want to make. But as a beginner who is looking to find a method to use that is simple and easy, then this is a good one to get started with.

The Shoulders and Head Patterns

Now it is time for us to move on to our third option to see how we are able to really make sure that we get some good results with our trading, and this is the head and shoulders pattern. This is a type of formation that you can notice on your graphs and charts that kind of looks like a baseline with three individual peaks. The two that fall on the outside should be similar in height, and then the one that falls right in the middle of them needs to be the highest.

This is a strategy that we are able to use in order to figure out if there is a trend reversal about to happen in the market or not. You can use it to see whether the trend reversal is bullish or bearish in nature as well. the pattern that you work with is going to include and be formed in three main parts, and all of them need t to be there to make sure that this trend works. The three parts that we need to spend some of our time on here to be prepared to use this strategy includes:

1. After the stock has gone through a bullish trend, you will see that the prices will reach a peak, and then there will be a decline. The decline that occurs is going to form a trough.
2. Then the price will rise again a little bit in order to form a second high, one that is actually quite

a bit above the first peak, but then it will decline down again.

3. The price will come back up a third time. but it won't go higher; it will simply go to the same height, or similar, as the first peak before it declines down once more.

The first and the third peak are going to be the shoulders, and the second peak is going to form the head. And then there is a line that will connect together the first and second troughs, and this is known as the neckline.

You will find that it is possible to work with this kind of trend in order to see whether there is a downward trend that is about to happen, and that can help you to know when the prices are about to go back down. If you are worried about the prices going down because you own some of the stocks, this is a great way to get out of the market and maintain your profits. But if you are trying to get into the market, you would want to look for one of these to tell whether it was a good time to enter the market or not.

Working With the Moving Average

The next option that we will take a look at is the moving average trend. This is a good one that helps us to know whether a security is about to go up or down, and can help us to see the best time to enter into a trade and the best time to get out. This is important because it is a good way to be prepared and come up with the plan that you want to use on a variety of different securities.

Remember that there are many stocks out there that you can choose from, and many of them will have their own morning trend that you can watch for, either going up or down really strong. You would then want to watch their charts and see where the moving averages head on the charts. This can be a beneficial thing to work with because the trader simply needs to watch these moving averages to learn more about how the trend is occurring. Then they can jump in at the right times and ride it out until they make profits.

While it is a strategy that takes a bit of time to learn and will require you to really watch the data that comes with it, you will find that this is one of the best options that you can choose to go with as well. There are a number of steps that we are able to follow in order to make this one work well, and some of them include:

- When you take a look at the graphs that you want to use, and you are checking out the stock you want to use, make sure that you look to see whether or not a trend is forming near the spot that is the moving average. When you do see this, you will want to get into the market and use this strategy. You can then spend a bit of time looking at the trading data that shows up for that stock from the day before. This is important to see how the moving average changes and how the stock is going to respond to that average.

- After looking over the charts, and getting a chance to see which moving average is the best one for the trade you are doing, it is time to make a purchase of the stock. Some traders do choose to wait a little bit longer in order to confirm the moving average before they enter. But either way, try to purchase as close to the lines for the moving average as you can.

- Once you are ready, you need to pick out the stop points that you want to use. You may want to consider setting the stop just a bit below the moving average line to help protect your investment, but it still allows for a little bit of volatility of movement. If you are doing this strategy with a candlestick chart, then you need to make sure that you have a start that is close to the moving average, and choose to work with a long position.

- After you have these in place and have been able to enter the market, you can just ride on that trend until you see the moving average break, and then take your profits.

When we handle this kind of strategy, we have to remember that we should not work with something known as a trailing stop. This is also a strategy where we need to pay and give our full attention to the market, and it is usually more than what the other strategies will ask for because it is possible that the market can move quickly, and it will get away from you. While the scanner is going to work well for helping you to get the right trades, we have to make sure that we are working with our own eyes, rather than relying on the scanner, especially when we work with this kind of strategy.

If you are looking at some of the charts and what they are telling us, and you see that the security you chose is going really far up from the moving average, this means that you are earning a good deal of profit. At this time, it may be in your best interest to take the half position rather than going to the full break. This will help you to walk away with some profits rather than nothing and can help you to avoid losing money if the trend decides to reverse itself. With the half position, if you reach it, you will still walk away with something

The Resistance Trading Method

Now it is time for us to dive right into our next strategy and how this will help us to take the stock market and earn a good profit on it. This is going to be one that will work with support and resistance and how we can harness those to make a lot of money. There are a bunch of other swing traders who work with this, so you will have some good company if you choose to go with it as well. The support is going to be what the price level is when the buyer is really strong, so strong that it is able to reverse or even interrupt a current downtrend that is on the graphs at that time.

When you are looking at a downtrend on the charts, and you notice that it gets to a specific support level, which is basically a place on the charts where the sock doesn't seem to get lower than at all, it will do a little bounce. The bounce is sometimes really big and sometimes really small, so it really depends on how the market is doing. When you look at your charts, you should see that this support line is going to be on the bottom, going horizontally, and it has to touch at least two of your bottoms before it can count.

In addition to spending some time on the support, we have to take a look at the resistance as well. this is going to basically be the opposite of what we talked about with the support bar. This is going to be the high price level that shows us that the position of selling is strong, one that is able to gain enough strength that it reverses the uptrend, at least a little bit.

Any time that you notice an uptrend get to this level, you should know that the trend is going to stop there, in most cases, and sometimes it will start to go down. Just like with the support, sometimes it will go down a lot and sometimes just a little bit. The resistance is something that is shown just like with the support, but it is able to connect two or more tops to it.

There are also some trading situations where it is possible to get support or resistance that is minor. These will cause a trend to pause a bit. But if you work with some of the major resistances and supports as we mentioned before, then this is strong enough to take our trend and force it into reverse. Traders who work with this strategy need to try and figure out how to purchase as close to the support as they can, and then they need to sell that position as close to the line of resistance as possible. This will be the best way to get the most profits out of that trade.

To make this strategy work, we need to figure out the levels of support and resistance. And to do this, we need to bring out a few daily charts that have our chosen stocks on this. Sometimes the line is a bit hard to find, and you need to look through a few days to see what is the best option and get a line that is clear enough you feel comfortable with using it. This means to get the most out of this trading strategy; you need to have some patience and keep your emotions in check.

Along with this, there are a few steps that we are able to use as long as we are able to pull out a few charts and graphs to help us get through this. Some of the steps that you can use to make this process easier and to make sure we get the most out of this strategy include:

- Remember talking about indecision candles at some point in your studies f swing trading? You are going to see these in areas of support and resistance. These candles often show that buys and sellers are fighting with each other to see who has the most control over the price.

- Often half dollars and whole dollars can be good support and resistance levels. This is especially true when you work on stocks under $10. If you can't find your support or your resistance lines, check here and see if your line would work there.

- When you make your own lines, you need to have the most recent data available. This ensures that you are getting the best information for that stock.

- The more that your line is able to touch the extreme price of the stock, the better option this line is for your support and resistance. If it is too far from this extreme point, then it is not going to have enough value to make it strong.

- Only look at any support or resistance lines that stay with the current price range. For example, if the stock's price is around $20 right now, you do not need to look at the region on the graph where the stock randomly jumped up to $40. This is not an area where the stock will probably go back to, so it doesn't make much sense to work from there.

- Many times the support and resistance are not just one exact number. Often it is more of an area. If you come up with a support or resistance that is about $19.69, then you know that the movement is somewhere near that number, not exactly that number. You can usually estimate that the area is going to be somewhere between five to ten cents above or under that line.

- The price that you want to work from will need to have a clear bounce off that level. If you can't find that this price bounces at that level, then this is not a good support or resistance level for you to work with. Your levels need to be really easy to notice and need to make sense of the charts you look at. If you have any questions about whether you picked the right one or not, it's not the right one.

When you head over to some of your charts and create the lines that you need for this strategy, it is easy to see that drawing the perfect line the whole time is a bit of a challenge. You have to use some caution when you pick the lines because there are so many variables, and you are basing all of your decisions on this as well. you need to go with the ones that make the most sense for your data, or you could really throw the work out.

The best way to do this is to get some practice. Look at a lot of different charts and graphs and get familiar with how they work and where the support and resistance would be. It is only as difficult as you make it, and the more practice you get with these, the easier it is to write in some of these lines that you can actually follow.

Opening Range Breakout

Another strategy that we can spend our time on is the opening range breakout. This is a good strategy because it does provide us with some good signals on when to enter the market, but sometimes there is an added challenge of knowing when you should get out of the process and take your profit. You do need to put in some elbow grease with this one and figure out the best place for this based on your own research, and you can even pick out how much profit you would like to make on the trade as long as it is realistic.

To work with this strategy, you have to really pay some good attention to what is happening in the market, and you have to be prepared to jump in right away. When you take a look at a few of the stock charts, you may see that a few of the socks in play (okay, most of them) are going to have some really violent price action in one direction or another.

The reason for this is that the buyers and the sellers are trying to flood into the market during the first few minutes when it is open. This is a crazy time for us to trade. New investors will often stay out of the market right here because there is a lot of volatility that shows up, and sometimes that is a lot for a beginner to handle.

However, as you get more experience with the market and learn more about how it works, it is possible to join in on this market rush and make some good money. If you are someone who panics with this, you need to be careful. It is a volatile time, and there are situations where you will be wrong and lose out on money in a short amount of time.

This is a time period where a lot of investors are going to panic and then sell their stocks because they think they need to regain their positions right away. Then there are some beginners who are not used to the market, and they will jump on as well for the discount or jump out because they are scared as well. both of these are important movements to watch because they will help us to get a better look at the price of the stock, and can tell us more about what will happen in the proceeding day as well.

Remember though all of this that you are working as a swing trader, it is usually best for you to stay out of the market and not jump into the opening range breakout. This is a method that can work, but it is so volatile, and it doesn't always go in the direction that you would like. Waiting about fifteen minutes, or a least a bit to see where the trend is settling down, is a much better option.

The reason that we want to wait a bit here is that it is so easy to get stuck in some of the craziness of the morning changes in the market, and you do not want to get the wrong ideas and get stuck on the wrong end of things either. You can wait just a few minutes, watching a few of the stocks that you favor, and still jump in without missing out on some of the great opportunities that will show up.

Like a lot of the other strategies that we have taken the time to talk about through our guidebook, the opening range strategy is going to work the best if you have some large stocks or mid-cap stocks that will not end up with some unpredictable price swings when you decide to hold onto them. You also want to be careful and not go with this strategy if you see some stocks that are low float. The best option is to choose stocks that can trade inside a range that is smaller than what we see with the Average True Range, or the ATR.

With some of that in mind, we need to walk through some of the steps that we can follow in order to get the most out of swing trading with this strategy. Some of the steps that we can use include:

- After you have had some time to create your watchlist in the morning, you should wait until the stock market has time to settle down, so wait for about five minutes. During this time, watch the price action and the opening range. You can also check out how many shares are traded during that time and then figure out from that information if the stock is going down or up. This time is when a ton of orders go through the market, and you want to look at these numbers to see how liquid a stock actually is.
- During this time, you can also look through to see what the ATR of that stock is. you want the opening range to be smaller compared to

the ATR, so make sure the ATR number is nearby.

- Once those first five minutes of market opening are finished, you may see that the stock will stay in that opening range a bit longer depending on what traders and investors want to do. However, if you see at this time that the stock is breaking out of this range, it time to enter the trade. Enter the trade going the same direction of the breakout. If you can, go long if you see the breakout is going up, but go short if the breakout is going down.

- Pick out a good target for your profit as well. You can find this by looking at the daily levels from the previous day and identify where the stock is before the market opens. You can also look at the previous days' close, along with the moving averages, to come up with a good target.

- If you can't find the right technical level for your chosen target or for the exit, you can choose to go long and then look for signs of weakness. On the other hand, if you want to take a short position, and then the stock goes high, this shows you the stock is strong, and you want to cover the position as much as you can.

This is a good strategy for a swing trader to work on if they want to have a short time frame, but it also works well with some of those longer time frames as well. Keep in mind here, that the steps we just went through above are done with some shorter trades that are only a day or two long. But it is simple enough to go through and expand it out a bit more to ensure you get the right amount of time for your trades.

The Interesting Red to Green Strategy

Now it is time for us to move on and take a look at a strategy that we can use known as the red to green strategy. The name of this one may sound a little funny, but it is a great option to make sure that you are prepared and can really catch some of the movements that will show up in your stocks. This strategy will require that you can look through some of the historical data that shows up for your stocks and then use that to figure out how you should react and which ways you should invest.

This one is going to have a really good look at some of the historical information because that is what will tell us what the stock has done in the past, and can give us a better idea of what it is likely to do in the future. While you are searching through some graphs and some of this historical data, it is important that you pay at least a little attention to some of the current prices of the stocks that you are interested in. If you do this and then notice that the price is higher than it was the day before, then this is a good indicator that the price is going up, and that will turn a green day over to a red day. What this will mean for us is that the percentage of the price change will end up being negative, and that shows up as red in our charts.

We can also take this the other way if we would like, which would mean that we go from a red to green day in some cases. It all depends on what information we are finding in our charts along the way.

The strategy that we have to work with here to make sure that our method works the way that we want, whether we go from green to red or red to green. To make this easier to understand, we will just stick with one of the options and look at the steps, and then you can make some adjustments to make sure that it works going the other way as well.

For this one, we will spend some time looking at how to go from a red to a green day, which is a common way to use this. To make sure that you use this strategy well, the steps that we have to follow will include:

- When you get up in the morning and are ready to start trading, and you are working on your watchlist, you need to make sure that you are pulling up information that comes from the previous day as well. Make sure that you specifically look at the closing information, checking out what the price action was at that time.

- If you see these chars and see that the stock is moving to where it was before on the previous close, this means that you will want to go along with that strategy. You can use your profit target from the previous day to set yourself up well.

- When setting up your stop loss on this strategy, you should be as close to the technical level as you can. This means that if you made a purchase at a support line, then make sure that the stop loss ends up being near where that support line was as well.

- It is also a good idea to come up with a profit target and then stick with it during the trade. It is going to help you to see the best results and will ensure that you can walk away with at least some sort of profit in the end.

This is a great strategy to work with if you have some of the historical data about your business, and you are excited to use it to your advantage. And you can definitely use it when the market is going in the other direction as well, which is going to make it one of the best strategies to learn because there is so much that we are able to do with it!

The Gap up, Inside Bar, and Then Breakout

The final one that we are going to work on here is a bit more complex than some of the others, but that is part of the fun of working with it as well. We are going to spend some time learning how to read the graphs with this one to ensure we see exactly what we think we do, and that way we can make some more in profits along the way. This is a trading signal that we work with, and you need to pull out the charts and see if there is some gap up in the process. Then, if you see that there is a second or a third ten-minute bar that also shows up here and it turns into what looks like an inside bar, you are set to go. This is going to be the setup that you need in order to make this particular strategy behave the way that you want.

Now, there are some traders who like to work with this particular strategy, but they make some changes to it. They will work with a few stocks that have a partial gap in place rather than one that has the full gap that we talked about. When we are on the search for that partial gap instead, you will need to look for a setup where the gap is higher than it was on the close for that stock on the previous day, or it is not going to work the way that we want.

In addition, we have to also make sure that the partial gap we are looking for will come in lower than the high of the previous day as well. the reason for this is that it will provide you with some good signals to show that this stock is a good one, but it also makes certain that along the way, you have a few good options to work with compared to waiting around for the full gap. You a choice whether you would like to work on the full gap or the partial gap, but the partial gap is sometimes seen as a safer alternative to work with.

When you are working with this strategy, you want to keep the charts to a minimum time frame. For example, you may only want to go with one or two of these ten-minute bars before you start with your inside bar. Beware though. If you see that there are more than these two ten-minute bars, it means that the price has had way too much movement at this point, and you should avoid this option because it isn't the most effective setup.

As soon as you have the right inside the bar, without too much volatility going on in the market, it is time to purchase your stop. Make sure that this stop is right about the high you see in your bar. The trigger is the breakout that is above your inside bar.

When you get to this point, it is possible that you need to be patient and wait a bit. We want to search around and find the right trade signal that can allow us to go long. Then, if you have your stop in place at the right time, you will need to think more about some of the logistics of your plan and how this will all work out. Keep it all in order and keep the stop loss points in the right place, and this strategy will work out great for you.

As we can see, there is a lot that we are able to love about working in swing trading, and there are a lot of great strategies that we can pick and choose from based on what meets our needs the best. When we can put all of this together, we can certainly use it to make some good profits in the stock market, or in any other market that we want, even as a beginner.

CHAPTER 7

TIPS TO GET THE MOST OUT OF THE SWING TRADING

Now that we have had some time to look at how to work in swing trading and all the great benefits that come with this, it is time for us to move on and look at a few of the different tips and tricks that we can use in order to see some great results. These tips will make sure that you can trade like a professional in no time, even if you haven't had a chance to work with swing trading or other types of stock market trading in the past. Some of the tips that we can follow to see the best results with our swing trading endeavors includes:

Pick Out a Stop Loss Point

One of the first things that you need to consider when working on some of your trades is where you would like to place your stop-loss points. There should be one that will pull you out of the market if the prices get too low and you start losing money, and then another one for the number of profits that you want to make, which will pull you out of the market when that number has been reached as well.

This needs to be as important to your plan as the entry point. These are your protections and will ensure that you are in and out of the market before you end up losing money and increasing your risk too much. The stock market, especially when it comes to swing trading, can be risky, so you have to learn how to cut that risk to a minimum as much as possible. These stop-loss points are going to be the best way to make this risk lower.

First, we want to set up our stop loss point for losing money. There are times when the market is not going to behave the way that we would like, and it turns downward, so we start to lose money. Our emotions can get into the mix and then we see our money slipping through our fingers. We get worried about this and we want to make the money back. So we stay in the market too long or we make some bad decisions, even if the charts and graphs are showing us exactly what we should do. We refuse to give up, and we may lose more money than necessary for this.

The stop loss point will help to prevent this kind of issue. You can set it right when you get in the market, thinking logically about how much money you would be comfortable losing on this trade if things don't go well. You will set this, and then if the market does reach that, it will kick your orders out, and you will get to regroup and restart later on. It is as simple as that and can help to reduce the amount of risk that you are dealing with along the way.

We also need to make sure that we place a stop loss in place for how much profit we can make as well. this may seem silly because we would all answer that we want to make as much money as possible, so why would we want to put one of these in place to limit our risk.

Unfortunately, it is not likely that the potential profit is going to be unlimited when we go with swing trading on the stock market, so that is not something that we should concentrate on at all. We need to always look at all trades and consider how much profits we would be happy with if the trade is successful. And then we need to put the stop loss there.

The way that this helps us is that it ensures we make some kind of profit if we enter the market and that we don't lose our profits in the process. It is too easy for us to get to the target profit, and then the market goes down, and we lose out on it all. This is another thing that the emotions can influence, and if we lose out on all of the profits, we will sure miss that profit instead. Add this in ahead of time to make sure that you can walk away from the trade with some profits.

Set Aside Money to Invest

It is important that you never invest money that you can't afford to use. It is easy to hear that there is a great option out there, one that you have to jump in right now, and you are guaranteed to make a lot of money on in the process. And so, because you trust that person so well and you know there is no way that you will lose, you put all of your savings and money towards the house on it and hope for the big money and the new lifestyle to come out.

But then things don't work out, and you end up losing a lot of money in the process. That big lead was all false, and the market takes a big turn. This is even more likely because you didn't take the time to learn about the market and what it can offer in the process. You lose everything, and now you are struggling to find money to pay the mortgage or any of the other things that you are hoping to get paid that month.

This is kind of extreme to think about, but it still shows us the importance of only investing what we can afford at the time. When you invest too much, or more than you can afford, then you will bring the emotions into the game, and that can be a dangerous thing to work with overall. It is much better to leave those emotions at the door or you make bad decisions that will lead you to failure.

Instead of investing money that you can' really afford, a better option to use is to set aside a separate savings account. The only money that goes into this account is the money that is for investing. It is not money that is earmarked to work for your mortgage, your insurance, your food, or anything else. It is extra money that is left in your budget and can be used for some of your investment without any worry about it being gone.

While none of us wants to lose money, of course, this is much safer to work with. Even if it is a small amount, it is money that is safe to play with and doesn't have any additional ties to it that you need to worry about. This means that you are able to use it, and if you are working on a strategy and it doesn't behave the way that you want, then the money won't be as big of a deal. Once the money is gone for that month out of the account, then you are done investing until the next month, or at least until you can put more money into the account. Don't let your investments cause you to live without, or you will end up with a lot of emotions in the process.

Keep the Emotions Out

The best thing that you can do when working on swing trading is to learn how to keep the emotions out of the game. Your emotions are going to be your worst enemy in all of this, and if you choose to add them in or you aren't able to block them out, then you will lose more money than you can ever make in the process. This is a hard one for a lot of people, and this is why many of them decide to not stick with trading at all.

The first thing to realize with this one is that you will lose money sometimes. Sometimes you will not understand what the market is doing, and you will make the wrong decisions. Sometimes you will not understand how to work with the strategy that you picked, and that can make you lose money. And sometimes the market just does something that no one was expecting and that makes a lot of investors, even those who are more experienced, lose money in the process as well.

If you have that realization in your mind from the start, then this can help you to stay calm and see some good results in the process. In fact, this is one of the best ways to make sure that when a loss happens, you will not be overwhelmed or feel like you need to stay in the market for too long. The stop-loss points that we talked about earlier will come in and make a big difference. They can get put in right at the beginning before you have a chance to let the emotions show up and cause some problems. Then the system will execute the plan or the strategy that you put in place, and it will help you to be situated and ready to go without all the emotions clouding your judgment.

Learn a Few Good Strategies and Stick With Them

We spent a lot of time in the previous chapter looking at some of the best strategies that you can use with swing trading, and really with lots of the trading methods that you want to use if you decide to branch out later. All of them work in slightly different manners, and it often depends on how the market is going, what the stocks are doing, and how much volatility is found in the market as a whole.

All of the strategies that we talked about in this guidebook are going to be legitimate ones that traders will use on a regular basis. This means that if you find the right market conditions, you can use any of them and earn some good profits in the process. There are times when they will fail, but this is more about the market moving in ways that you were not expecting, and not that there is something wrong with this strategy in the first place.

This means that you have a lot of really great options that you are able to work with, ones that will make it so much easier for you to figure out how the market is working and how you can make money. There are even options that will work well whether you want to look for an upward trend or the downward trend in the market at the time. You have to choose which works for you.

As a trader, the market is going to change on you quite a bit, so you need to have at least a handful of options available that you are comfortable with. This will greatly expand your reach in the market and can help you to be prepared for all kinds of market conditions based on what works the best at that time. The more of these you know how to do, the better as well. But working with just a few of them at a time, and then expanding out to more as you gain more familiarity, can really make a big difference as well.

You can choose any of thee strategies that you would like to work with. There are many in the previous chapter that can help you to get into the market at the right time to see some results. You can also look and do some of your research in order to find some of the ones that you would like. But pick out two or three options that you are comfortable with using and work from there to get the best results in the process with your trading and to help you prepare for all kinds of situations.

Don't Switch Strategies While In a Trade

One thing that we need to remember is that when we enter into a trade, we need to stick with it. This can be hard. Many beginners will get started with a trade, and insist on switching to a new strategy that they didn't start with in the first place. This is one of the worst things that you can do for your success in the stock market, so you have to avoid it.

If you go through and find that one of the strategies you are using is not providing you with any success, then this is a sign that it is time to get out of the trade and get out of it. This is hard sometimes. We want to work with a strategy that is going to win. But sometimes, even the best traders end up losing money, and you need to know when it is time to get out and try something else. Sometimes a strategy will not work the way that we want, and we just need to get out and try a new trade later on.

It is really easy for a beginner to get into the trade and then not follow this rule. They see a trade that looks good and like it would work well with the strategy that they picked. But after they get in the market, things reverse and don't work the way that they want. Then they will go through and try to switch their strategy and try out a few other things. Whether they just wing it along the way or they pick out another strategy instead, they make changes right in the middle of the trade. This will barely go well for you.

Changing your strategy is never a good thing to work with at all. This is just asking for things to go wrong. You are not planning things out and thinking it through when you do this, and that can lead to some dangerous trades that will keep you from making the money that you want in the process. Even if the trade does not go the way that you want, it is best to start with one trade and stick with it until the trade is done.

When that trade is done, you can always go back and try a different strategy later on.

There are a lot of options that you are able to work with for swing trading. This is very important to understand, and you have to learn which one works the best for the market conditions that you see. But never go through and switch from one strategy to the next when you are already doing a trade.

These tips are going to be so important to ensure that we are going to get the best results overall here. It is hard to get into the stock market, especially when we work with a shorter-term option like swing trading. You need to make some smart decisions, you need to make sure that your emotions are not getting in the way, and you need to think through all of the decisions that you do at the time. When you are ready to get into the market, and you want to see how great it can be for your needs, make sure to follow these tips to help improve your rate of success.

CONCLUSION

Congratulation on making it through to the end of Swing Trading, let's hope it was informative and able to provide you with all of the tools you need to achieve your goals whatever they may be.

The next step is to jump right in and get ready to do some of the tradings on your own. We took a lot of time to look more at this kind of investment strategy and what we are able to do with it as well. this is a simple strategy, and it can really bring in a ton of results. But sometimes looking through all of this information can be a challenge, and figuring out where to start is not always as simple as it seems.

The goal here is to help show you how easy swing trading can be and why it is one of the best options to make sure that you are set and ready to go when it is time to put your money to work for you. We went through the steps that are necessary to get the trade going, as well as a lot of the different strategies that you can use along the way to make sure you get in and out of the market at the right times.

There are going to be sometimes when you lose money. That is just the way that this process works, and even those who have been in the market for a long time will be able to lose on occasion. As you get more practice with swing trading and the strategies that you like to use, you will find that this process gets better, and you will get more wins overall.

Swing trading is one of the best options that you can use when it is time to invest your money and put it to work for you. When you are ready to learn more about swing trading and what it can do for you, make sure to check out this guidebook to get started.

Finally, if you found this book useful in anyway, a review on Amazon is always appreciated!

www.ingramcontent.com/pod-product-compliance
Lightning Source LLC
Chambersburg PA
CBHW071432210326
41597CB00020B/3756

* 9 7 8 1 9 5 1 3 4 5 4 0 2 *